Crossing the Phantom River

CROSSING
THE PHANTOM RIVER

James Masao Mitsui

THE GRAYWOLF PRESS
PORT TOWNSEND, WASHINGTON

Some of these poems first appeared in the following anthologies and periodicals: *Poetry Northwest*, *The New York Quarterly*, *Pacific Search*, *Raven*, *The Pacific*, *Waterfront Review*, *Slackwater Review*, *Greenfield Review*, *Grove*, *Chariton Review*, *Mundus Artium*, *Journal of Ethnic Studies*, *Footprint*, *Pacific Poetry & Fiction Review*, *Tides: A Vision of Contemporary Japanese American Art*, *The Washington Review*, and *The Willow Springs Magazine*.

Cover art by Alan Chong Lau.

The author and publisher would like to thank the National Endowment for the Arts for its support.

Published by The Graywolf Press, PO Box 142, Port Townsend, WA 98368.

for Suzanne Elizabeth

CONTENTS

I. Exhibition of Archaeological Finds

PAINTING BY A MENTAL PATIENT, WEAVERVILLE,
CALIFORNIA, JAIL 1922   3
FROM A FACTORY WINDOW, 1904   4
EXHIBITION OF ARCHAEOLOGICAL FINDS OF THE
PEOPLE'S REPUBLIC OF CHINA, ASIAN ART MUSEUM,
SAN FRANCISCO   5
DREAMING ABOUT DAYLIGHT   6
AFTER A PAINTING BY HSIA KUEI   7
SAMURAI   8
WATERFALL AT DUSK   9
LANDSCAPE WITH SNOW   10
LI PO RIDING HIS DONKEY   11
SURROUNDED BY AUTUMN   12

II. Under the Killdeer Cry

BACKYARD   15
CEREMONY   16
AMTRAK, SEATTLE TO PORTLAND, VALENTINE'S DAY   17
POEM WITH 36 LINES   18
THE RAYONIER COMPANY PARK AT ROCKAWAY, OREGON   19
TWO HONEYMOONS   20
PREPARED CHILDBIRTH CLASS   21
SHREVE, CRUMP & LOW COMPANY AD IN *The New Yorker*   22
THE BEACH AT ONA, OREGON COAST   23
LETTER TO HUGO FROM KALALOCH   24
QUINAULT RIVER   25
CAPE ALAVA   26

III.   From the Banks of the Skykomish

KATORI MARU, OCTOBER 1920   29
WAR MEMORY   30
HOLDING CENTER, TANFORAN RACE TRACK, SPRING 1943   31
BLOCK 18, TULE LAKE RELOCATION CAMP   32
KAMIKAZE, THE DIVINE WIND   34
FROM THE BANKS OF THE SKYKOMISH   35
WHEN FATHER CAME HOME FOR LUNCH   37
OUTHOUSE IN LAMONA   38
ALLOWANCE   39
ICE SKATING ON COFFEE POT LAKE   40
REGRET   41
THE TABLE LAMP MY SISTER ORDERED OUT OF THE
MONTGOMERY WARD CATALOG AND GAVE TO MY
MOTHER FOR CHRISTMAS, 1949   42
MONDAY NIGHT, AFTER CORRECTING PAPERS   43
FOR A CHINESE PHEASANT   44

IV.   The Dream Ritual

FREEDOM   47
AFTER HEARING THAT THE OLD BROADWAY HIGH
SCHOOL HAS BEEN TORN DOWN   48
5:45 FERRY TO SEATTLE   49
EVICTION NOTICE   50
AFTER A LETTER FROM RANSOM   51
FISHING IN EAGLE HARBOR WITH GARRETT HONGO   52
OUTSIDE THE DREAM RITUAL   53
LINES FOR FORTUNE COOKIES   54
FOR THE BALLERINA IN THE MOJAVE DESERT WHO
HAS PAINTED HER OWN AUDIENCE ON A CANVAS AND
STRETCHED IT, FACING THE STAGE   55

I

Exhibition of Archaeological Finds

Painting by a Mental Patient, Weaverville, California Jail, 1922

—now displayed in the Weaverville Museum

It is the picture of a man who dreams
at night, his dreams a color
he can't forget in his blue cell.
A fork chases a hard-boiled egg
across the smooth paper,
watched by an angry alarm clock.
The clock rings
and the artist knows it is morning
even though the iron cell
is in a basement with no windows.

In the middle of the painting
the devil blows a whistle
and his pitchfork drips blood.
Above in the night
a man has taken off in a rocket
heading for a yellow, one-eyed moon.
He grips the steering wheel in the open cockpit
and never looks back.

In a quiet corner
under a naked tree
a satyr sits & plays his pipes.
The music weaves all around the painting,
twists around a girl
dancing in veils.

The man who dreams all this
pulls at his covers,
sleeps at the bottom of the painting.

The man who painted this
died in his dreams.
The painting of his dreams
rests on an easel
in the dim museum corner.
Past closing time, past the turning out
of lights, the people in the painting
listen to their own noise.

From a Factory Window, 1904

A cracked leaf
hangs in a fluttering spider web
outside the sill.
She has slipped over
to the high
south window.
Stands tiptoe & peeks
through the boards.
Two men are playing golf.
It's Sunday.
The young girl
doesn't understand the small
white ball, only
that the raw gears of her spinning
machine must not bind.
Already, without her feeding,
it begins to whine.

Exhibition of Archaeological Finds of the People's Republic of China, Asian Art Museum, San Francisco

Inside a humidified glass case
a bronze horse
uses momentum to stay upright.
The guards keep reminding me
no photographs can be taken
of its sharp but aging ears,
open nostrils, mouth & full teeth.
Its silent green coat
looks brushed smooth by wind.
As I watch
it proves its speed,
one earthbound hoof
stepping on a swallow in full flight.

Dreaming about Daylight
—for Edward Sheriff Curtis (1887-1952)

Five horsemen ride under a cactus moon,
closely wrapped in trading blankets
& half-light. They are riding away,
their backs dark as their own shadows,
the shadows of Joshua trees
along the trail. The figures
are dreaming about daylight.
Just now I notice
one has looked back.
Back at a sunrise
& a photographer
given the spirit of sun & stars.

After a Painting by Hsia Kuei (1190-1225)

A man & a woman stand at a last
wide step. Above them
vine maples twist
& cling to a cliff
like tenacious scholars.
Crows gather in the madronas.
Sweets & delicate tea
wait under the lanterns. Below
in the valley
fog sweeps across a river.
Men drink wine and sing,
beating time
on the side of their boat.

I hold the painting up to a window.
Two Canada geese fly from the east,
drift into the silk, the slanting rain.

Samurai
—for Miyamoto Musashi

The same hand
that pauses in the autumn sky
to paint wind
whispering through bamboo,
joins the other hand
on the long hilt of a naked sword
& cuts a man in half
at the thighs,
leaving behind a pair of bloody wheels:
skin, flesh, bone & marrow.

Waterfall at Dusk
—after a painting by Shin-gei (1431-1485)

The ivory columns of
a waterfall
arch
next to a bamboo house
under a hanging cliff.

A rushing sound
saturates the air.

Below the foam of the falls
an old monk
with attendant
taps with his cane
before crossing the bridge.

Landscape with Snow
—after a painting by Li T'ang (1050-1130)

Wind stirs the surface
of the lake, shakes the trees
& grass, whips at the fisherman
balanced in the bow
of his boat. Ink
blends across the silk, silver waves
ruffle & snap their backs.

We feel the weather, feel pity
for the man
who buys each day
by selling his frozen catch
from his boat. The painter
pulls at his white beard
and says he's only the presence
that animates the water.
He says this,
reciting poems under his breath.

Li Po Riding His Donkey

Foothills cross in the blue
haze & drifting clouds
of Chinese mountains.
People in the village
have listened to his latest poem.
It has taken two hours
and a gallon of sake.
They sing in their small houses
and repeat the thrill
of ten thousand rivers.

Li Po stops at a crossing,
leaves his crooked mount.
He wades out, embraces
the reflection of the moon.
It whispers to him
what he's been listening for
all his life. His face
floats away, scatters in the rapids.

Surrounded by Autumn

A stone bridge
crosses the top
of a waterfall,

a path
where a man
in a white robe

cleans the ground
with a broom
of ricestalks.

Wild geese
sweep down to a sandbar.
The man

shakes a branch
and decorates the stones
with maple leaves.

II

Under the Killdeer Cry

Backyard

Her lace petticoat floats on the line.
Barn swallows twirl
and skid in the sky like musical notes.
Bare almond trees
bend to the rhythm of the wind.
A branch
slithers against the side of the house.

I kneel in the wet grass
and pick up the seat to the swing.
Replace it.
The storm hurtles across a far hill.
I am alone in the light of a wide moon.

Ceremony

The long distance phone
clenches my heart
like a fist. I fall
into darkness, a pit
of splintered bones.
My heartbeat attacks,
attacks, your rape
slashes me like a razor
inch deep, wrist to elbow.

This bath I give you,
this cleansing,
starts to wear away
the memory. Washing
the clotted blood
from your blonde hair
I notice your left ear
split by the butt of his gun.
The last of the tangled blood
is too close to your temple.

Bruises tighten my eyes
into sharp edges, tighten
my fists with no place
to go. Wounds float
in our minds
like stars in a deep ocean.

AMTRAK, Seattle to Portland, Valentine's Day

I picked them straddling a ditch
along the county road—
the pussywillows,
stems tight in a rubber band,
relax in waxpaper.
They wait on the seat
beside me, half the 200 miles between us
almost gone. The moon
drops from the sky,
races on the river along the tracks.
Lights of farmhouses
blur past like watered fabric.
My breath changes to a whisper.

Poem with 36 Lines

This is the second line of this poem.
The first asks
not to imagine an elephant
when you hear the word *elephant*.
Some people deny this,
that's why I know it is there
like a mime's piano
pushed to the edge of a stage.

An artist paints shingles
clinging to a building
to stay away from boredom.
Below him
dancers move in a skylight,
building rhythms
where there was emptiness.
They fill blank spaces
in the painting.

A Nebraska scarecrow
wears expressive suspenders.
I've never seen him
but he stands there
tall as a man.
Here in Washington
a plastic owl waits on a span
of the East Channel Bridge
and scares away 99 per cent
of the pigeons. Highway departments
believe in efficiency.

Tonight on a Thursday
the moon has moved back
where it belongs, open
and hanging over invisible mountains.
I stand in front of our bedroom mirror.
It contains your absence.
I touch the flattened room.

The Rayonier Company Park at Rockaway, Oregon

I'm sitting in a photograph
on a baggage wagon. The steam engine
at my back does not run,
stands on a discontinued spur.
Across the tracks
it is Garibaldi, Oregon.
Back by our car
on a table under bony alders
our picnic basket waits: red wine,
a French loaf and cracked crab.
The woman at the fish market
on the highway called us lucky,
yesterday the crabs were so fresh
& excitable they would have shaken off
their legs in the boiling water.
My eyes are stopped by a red & white
Railway Express Agency sign
nailed to the siding of the small depot.
Your breath drifts toward me in clear focus.

Two Honeymoons

1

Love is the soaring of two eagles,
always two,
floating in close circles
above broken cliffs & twisting roads.
Driving California Highway 1
south of the redwoods,
pale grassland hills rise from the coast.
Poppies grow wild in the rocks.
Resting by a smooth stream,
reflections dance on your face.

2

Our neighbors have been gone
on their honeymoon for a week.
Their second car is parked by the stairs
to the marina next door.
Balloons wrinkle obscenely
on the bumpers. Letters spelling
"just married" have run down the windshield
in the heat. Two white signs in the side
windows stare at people and say,
"X-ray technicians know
all the positions," and "This car
stops at every hotel, motel
and flat rock." Passers-by cheer.

Prepared Childbirth Class

Membrane-white gloves
lift a plastic bag, the placenta
slips out, slides like liver
across the tray. Just a bit
of blood, she says, that took
its sweet time
draining from the tissues.
Yours will be clean, pink,
not deep red like this.

I keep swallowing back
the tomato juice we had
at the break, hold tight hands
with my pregnant wife and look back:
the placenta has hemispheres.
Two arteries and a vein
course like blue rivers
across one side.
The umbilical twists
like a limp hose.
She shows us the amniotic sac
tears easily, pokes a hole
with a finger and pulls it apart.
Twice she asks someone to pull up
her sleeves, the white cuffs
roll away from the blood.
We whisper our questions.

Shreve, Crump & Low Company Ad in *The New Yorker*
—*for Helen Bedteylon*

Shown actual size
the pendants: diamond in white gold,
sapphire & diamond in platinum,
ruby & diamond in yellow gold,
ruby & diamond in platinum,
take up a full column
in *The New Yorker*. These hearts
cost $600 to $2000 each,
adding tax where applicable.

They have been jewelers in Boston
since 1800. I have been a lover
of oceans since I was born.
On clear nights at Rialto Beach
the moon is tied to a rope
the color of the water.
Under the killdeer cry
you can hear the wash of rocks
rolling back into the waves
like jewels
cupped in the hands,
tossed back
just for the sound.

22

The Beach at Ona, Oregon Coast

You can see the wind blow
the way the trees
shape themselves away from the ocean.
At Cape Foulweather
we read a historic marker
about Captain James Cook
using all the rope on board his ship
to find the bottom of the Pacific,
the end of his imagination.

Along this twisting gray coast
rollers continue to tear off their crests.
Far from the lights of winter cities
we sleep in our car,
understand the rumor of the waves.

Letter to Hugo from Kalaloch

Dear Dick. I turned that corner this morning in Copalis
Beach, the one that pulls tourists over at Chuck's
Chili Bowl, and seeing that skinny nylon-legged
waitress in a brown uniform washing the plate glass
window facing the ocean like it was her only job,
I thought of you. Your letters full of Montana
and echoes of this Washington coast, persuaded me
to write. Out here where rivers end and clouds are giant
roads, I find assurance in the flashing light
on Destruction Island. Rye bread gleams
with melted butter on the kitchen counter in cabin 15.
Outside, children run across the satin-wet sand,
the wind brushing their hair long. In the light
of a sun waiting on the horizon, Suzanne sits
on pillows on the daybed and reads into a book of letters
by Sylvia Plath. Our talk echoes as the ocean breathes.
She tells me horsetail shots can heal nettle burns,
that some wounds never heal, are hidden
like Hoh Head and the Giants' Graveyard
tucked in clouds to the north. High tide begins
to pile waves against the sandstone bank below our cabin,
flings water in the face we found carved in rock
by piddock clams, floats the driftwood snakes & birds
we named this afternoon. On Beach 4 we turned
along the shore and laughed at the drunken tracks
following us. You & Ripley watched from one
of the two trollers standing offshore, past the rocks.
Holding our laughs we danced across the tumbled
backs of prehistoric gray logs, heading for the shadow
of the trailhead. Tourists limped down the beach
carrying cardboard boxes of driftwood; Dick,
I had you following them, cracking a kelp whip
and the sinewy lines of your poems against their backs.

Quinault River
—for Steve Jaech

Eating in the car: cold beer,
roast beef tucked in a French roll,
I watch a boy give up fishing,
squirting fish eggs
between his fingers
at the invisible salmon
under the bridge
in the whispering river.

Tar-patched cracks
stitch the road, shine in the evening,
the late sun
after the rain.
Your fish stories
wrap around me like wool
army blankets. North on 101
crossing the Hoh, the Bogachiel,
the Elwha, this river country
surrounded by hills
greener than money, I agree
with the old woman in the Seattle
drugstore who held up a $2 bill
and said, "These are dangerous!"

Cape Alava

Past Almstrom's Prairie
the deer trail to the beach
is covered by thick
expressive cedar planks.
For three miles we hike,
a rhythm in line,
listening for the empty
shell sound of the ocean.
Mudhens take off from a deep
pool, leaving circles
that ripple into clay banks.

Breaking into the open
we face a ripping wind
and stand still as tree bark
to read the carving of stone
& wave. Winter tides
roll the petroglyphs
like stone dice.
Out there, over the waves,
there are no defeating hills.

III

From the Banks of the Skykomish

Katori Maru, October 1920

Two weeks across a strange sea,
big waves, the ship
spilling its toilets.
People sick of the ocean
run from bulkhead to bulkhead,
trying to keep their balance
on the slick iron deck.

My mother asks herself in Japanese
why her oldest sister had to die,
why now she must marry the stranger
who speaks Japanese & English
and swears with the crew.
She thinks back to Nagano-ken,
pictures her mother
cracking a brown egg
over a bowl of rice
while her father washes raw soil
from his thick hands.
Today she could trade her future
for the bottom of the ocean.

Waves, floating waves,
rise above the railing,
drift out of sight. Vancouver Island
is a memory of home, hills
soft & green as crushed velvet.

In Tacoma, Minoru buys
Western clothes: a pink taffeta dress
full of pleats, wide-brimmed hat,
white gloves, a leather handbag
and awkward high heels.
No more flowered silk,
obi sash and getas.
He brings out a used coat from the closet,
thick maroon wool, brown fur collar.
It is too full in the shoulders,
the size & color
fit her sister.
But for now she accepts it.
The rain feels heavy
on the gray sidewalks of America.   29

War Memory
—for Kay Deeter

In Richland
you open a door on your mother.
She looks up
like she's hiding a present.
Says she's just putting
your Japanese doll away
until the war is over.
Carefully it is placed
in its lacquer & glass case
and stored in a heavy box.
You escort your mother
and the doll
up the attic stairs
saying, "Good-bye, good-bye,"
in the ceremony in your mind.

Holding Center, Tanforan Race Track, Spring 1942
—for Miné Okubo

Dinner was cold: one boiled potato,
a can of Vienna sausage
and rice with cinnamon & sugar.
Outside the fence
a dog barks in the cricket-filled night.
You stay in your horse stall,
sitting on a mattress stuffed with straw
and stare at white grass
growing up through the floor.
Hay, horse hair & manure
are whitewashed to the boards.
In the corner
a white spider is suspended
in the shadow of a white spider web.

Block 18, Tule Lake Relocation Camp
—for James I. Ina

1

The emotion of trucks, buses & troop trains
brings them here,
to the wrong side of another state.
A woman at the Klamath Falls depot
calls it the wrong side of the ocean.

2

Crumbs hide around table legs
in the messhall,
dishes & silver
clink a strange song.
Families talk across long tables.
Questions drop like puzzles
to the unfinished floor.

3

Blocks away from their new home
a woman finds a latrine
not backed up. Stands
in line, waiting her turn
in the wind. Down
the center of the open room:
12 toilet stools, six pair,
back to back. Sits down
and asks for privacy
holding a towel in front of her
with trembling hands.

4

In a North Dakota prisoner-of-war camp,
surrounded by Germans & Italians,
a quiet man
hammers a samurai sword from scrap metal
at night in a boiler room.
A secret edge
to hold against the dark mornings.

He sends love notes to his pregnant wife
in Tule Lake
sewn in pants
mailed home for mending.
His censored letter
mentions a torn pocket.
She finds the paper near the rip,
folded & secret in the lining.

White voices
claim the other side of the ocean
is so crowded
the people want to find death
across the phantom river.
Headlines shake like nervous words.
Out on the coast
beach birds print their calligraphy
in the sand.
It is a small country.

Kamikaze, the Divine Wind

*—written on the 30th anniversary
of the bombing of Nagasaki*

1. 1274 & 1281

Twice Kublai Khan stands on Kyushu
at the edge of victory
& twice the clouds stand high
over the East China Sea.
A Sea Dragon gathers the divine wind
& blows a typhoon
at the Mongols. The Great Khan
turns back to the mainland,
through his scattered fleet,
through the tangled waves & divine wind
painted across six panels
of a folding screen.

2. 1945

Kamikaze echoes on planes over Okinawa,
on ships & islands in the Pacific.
Radios play with the word
in barbershops, in foreign parlors.
But the breath of ten thousand men
does not cause a wind.
Tokyo dies in a firestorm
left by a thousand planes.
The skin of victims
scrapes like charred toast in the ruins.
No wind can cool them.

In New Mexico
the desert turns to glass
at the point of explosion.
Sagebrush flats 20 miles away
change to scorched stubble.
A red sun sets
& casts a pattern in the Mojave clouds
like the Japanese flag.

From the Banks of the Skykomish

1. WINTER, '72

Big rocks explode the river,
close to where the house I was born in
was torn down after the War.
So close to the Great Northern tracks
I got used to pounding floors
that breathed deep.
That morning in '42 caught me too young
to ask why we had to leave Skykomish,
why the relocation camp was cold,
our barracks walls so thin & public.

2. EARLY SPRING JOURNAL ENTRY

The night fills with thunder.
Crickets sing in the alfalfa
along the old highway.
A fish under the railroad bridge
breaks the surface,
shatters it like a mirror.
Bubbles trail under a silver wind,
blossoms of Indian plum
spin by in the current.
A man turns from the railing
and heads down the tracks,
away from his dark house.
Cross-ties define his steps.

3. SUMMER IN A FRIEND'S CONDEMNED APARTMENT

A cot fits the shape
of my back. Things hard
are not always bad.
I've quit asking why people change.
Only a man who sleeps 15 months
in a friend's kitchen
knows the reason.

4. Fishing the Skykomish on a Fall Weekend with My Children

We spend a warm day unsnarling lines,
tying hooks and crimping sinkers.
My son keeps looking for a better place,
tells with wide arms about a salmon
someone just caught on the other side.
The girls only care about the fish
they can see in the shallows.
Just want to see how they're doing.
Britt disagrees, says the bigger the river,
the deeper the bottom,
the bigger the fish.

5. First Page of a Journal, Winter '73

Lines reach endlessly in the dark.
Are the storms out there
like the dust storms back home?
The sky turned brown as a gunnysack
and I kneeled at the wide
living room window. Days tumbled by
like Russian thistles.
Once I shattered that window
with a tight fist. Blood
curled from the crease between my finger
& thumb. Down to my wrist
held like a bracelet
as I settled on the floor
against a forgiving wall.

Thoughts flutter like clothes
on a line. Outside,
a chainsaw cries through a stand
of twisted Chinese elms.
I pinch a scar, remember the pain.

When Father Came Home for Lunch

I listen to my parent's language,
watch my father eat his separate meal,
the railroad motor car
cooling off and waiting
on the siding by the section house.
He sits with his back to the burning
woodstove in a captain's chair
and eats the family left-overs,
a bowl of rice balanced in his hand,
chopsticks flicking
around to the bowls & dishes
arranged in front of him.

Mother adds fried onions, a fried egg
and potatoes to his main bowl.
He adds catsup, shoyu
and mixes it with the white radish,
egg plant and cold chicken.
He works around to the mustard caked bowl
before each mouth of rice,
sauce hanging from his mustache.
Hot coffee, heavy with sugar & cream,
steams from a china mug.
Half-an-hour of noisy manners
and he's gone, back to work
in oily bib overalls.
I can still smell sweat
soaking his long-sleeved workshirt.

Outhouse in Lamona
"Everyone should write an outhouse poem"
(—*Nelson Bentley*)

I smell nappa, green onions & Haug's cow manure
from our garden.
It is too dark to read.
The wind is too slow
to shake the leaves of the cherry tree.
Crickets & frogs
are clear music
under the silent sunflowers.

Before going back in the house
I climb the locust tree.
Sit in a high limb, naked.
Too hot to sleep.

Allowance

I am ten.
My mother sits in a black
rocking chair in the parlor
and tells stories of a country school
surrounded by ricefields
and no roads.

I stand in the kerosene light
behind her,
earning my allowance.
A penny
for each white hair I pull.

Ice Skating on Coffee Pot Lake

The ice echoes
and I remind myself that at zero
it can hold a truck.
Sliding out on leather soles
I test the stillness,
see water dogs stir mud
under my feet.

Back on land
I sit on a frozen fence post
and pinch my toes & thick socks
into my brother's tired skates.
The laces are heavy.

Out on the lake
I skate to a place where I stop,
look back.
The sooty smoke of our fire
snakes itself into the sky
above the gray sagebrush shore.

Regret

My father watered his thick garden
summer evenings, nighthawks
slipping in the sky above the willows.
Straight rows of cabbage & pole beans
grew longer each year.
Cucumbers & egg plant
spread into neighboring lots.

We brought U-Haul trailers
and moved my mother to Seattle.
We decided what she wouldn't need.
What didn't fit we left behind.
Buried my father's urn
300 miles from his garden.

The Table Lamp My Sister Ordered out of the Montgomery Ward Catalog and Gave to My Mother for Christmas, 1949

My mother's hands are not hers
anymore, she's left them back home
almost 30 years ago in Lamona.
I keep wanting to see the strong fingers
that plucked chickens
just axed by my father, that wrung out
over-alls above a tub & washboard. Those hands
juggled three oranges or ripped away
the crabgrass choking the blue irises.
Now they're spotted with age, thin,
belong on a bird. After work
when I stop to visit
she shows me a dark bruise, a lump
on her forearm where she'd only had
a blood test. We talk more
with our eyes as her small tv
plays like a silent movie in color.
She offers me a mug of coffee,
cookies bought on her Monday shopping trips
downtown. I can only recall her sick
one day, thinking back to when I was a kid.
It was a strength that carried her
five weeks across the ocean,
and past the deaths of two sons
I never knew, one drowned in two inches
of a pond. When I leave she gives me
things to take home, keep for her.
This time it's a brass lamp.
Coming across the Sound in a ferry,
I slump in my car, stare across waves
torn out of a Hokusai print.
Mountains rest on the horizon in jagged silence.

Monday Night, after Correcting Papers

I'm dragging the river
tonight, poems
like bodies
tangled in the silt,
anchored by car tires,
bed springs & old radiators.
Hair & moss
drift with the sluggish current,
wave downstream
at channel bottom.

Giving myself a break
I step over to the doorjamb,
rub my back like my father
and shout his, "Cock-sacca!"
at the apartment.
He was a poet the way he drank.

For a Chinese Pheasant

Remembering the bright fabric of feathers,
the blue-green shine,
the sleeping eyes,
the tailfeathers with black stripes,
I tear off a single piece of meat
and chew away the dark taste.

IV
The Dream Ritual

Freedom

Sunlight falls under the pergola.
Pigeons dance awkwardly
in & out of shadow,
eager for the torn heels
of day-old restaurant bread.
The man is satisfied,
now it's thirst
that makes him hungry.
The cast-iron drinking fountain
doesn't work past a leak,
wet clay
pools in a depression and smells
of chlorine. I can't escape the red
bead eyes of the birds, the men,
until I reach 2nd & James.
Wind brushes puddles
floating in the brick gutter.
I smell a bakery in the wind.
The rest of the day
is my own.

After Hearing that the Old Broadway High School Has Been Torn Down

A late spring wind
brushes white waves across the restless
Sound. On the opposite shore
a stick-figure
turns in the dawn
and stands in a field of questioning yellow iris.

Downtown in straight glass buildings
with mirrors for windows,
businessmen look at what they've done,
say it's good
we've lost the structure of how we lived.
Their scale models
are clean as libraries with no books.

The old buildings keep leaving,
silent as Charlie Chaplin.
Stone lions
fall on marble steps.
There is no music in the wrecking ball,
the twisting pipes,
the shattering brick & plaster.
White dust
swirls from the jagged ends of hallways.

5:45 Ferry to Seattle

A plover skips a line toward shore,
the creosote plant in Eagle Harbor.
Up the cobbled beach, tucked
between two piers, I check our green
house. Imagine you on the porch,
holding Tadao, watching me off to work.
Turning toward Seattle, Mount Rainier,
white snow, pink in the southeast morning,
swings starboard. A reflection
flashes orange across the Sound
from a house on Alki. Someone
has opened a window, smelled the salt air.

Five minutes out on Elliot Bay
the *Walla Walla* crosses waves left by a freighter
heading for Asia.
Amber lights flicker from barricades on 2nd Avenue
where two men are sleeping
in a doorway, waiting for me to walk by.
Behind me, workers ask each other
if they've worked those new
Japanese or Italian tool machines yet.
They sit next to their black lunchpails
and laugh about the directions.
The oldest voice
notices Rainier sticking up,
says he keeps his eye on the background.
When the buildings line up across the horizon
it's time for him to leave.
Right now, it's still
another day, another 50 cents.

In the booth ahead
a man in a gray sweater,
with sailboat hair,
is busy printing red directions on a blueprint
that keeps wanting to roll up. Outside,
the Smith Tower,
the tallest building in the West when I was a kid,
is sinking into the city.

Eviction Notice

They sit heavily on unmade beds
under naked droplights
and watch dim TV.
They cough. They wear frayed tennis shoes,
undershirts, wide suspenders
& a dress hat.
They keep cats in their room.
They play dominoes
on bare plywood tabletops
and never keep score.
They carry canes. They tape
paper U.S. flags on the wall.
They keep a coffee can of flowers
on their bureau
beside a framed picture
of chrysanthemums & fruit.
They look at themselves in the mirror
and never smile, make fists
that still look young.

After a Letter from Ransom

Knowing you are out there, spreading poetry
in places like Raymond,
taking meals at cafe counters
surrounded by clear
cut hills & people who haven't read a poem
in ten, twenty years
I feel better. Outside
alders dance in a wet wind.

I think of a student I didn't know,
dead a month now, thrown
from a motorcycle. Posters for a benefit
dance kept his name a refrain
in the hallways for a week.
Then it slipped away.
I think of a girl's poem
confirming his work, his unfinished
clay pipes left on a workbench
in a pottery class. It is her best
poem, she knows his absence
better than his face.

Sometimes I work & work students
for poems, covered with chalk,
full of ideas, voice thinning
late in the day and it's still
that quick 10-liner they come up with
that's best. It's good to witness
this, our presence, the order
we try to create & continue.

The way we are serious
about our lives is important, the world
listens in sometimes
and it's not bad to be lost here
even when I hear my book
has been found in a second-hand
bookstore. That's how we grow,
that's why we overhaul old boats,
keep them standing by
for the best crabbing tide of the year.

Fishing in Eagle Harbor with Garrett Hongo

You've left your phone unhooked
across the Sound—
actors & secretaries call a busy number.
Today we need to fish, talk about baseball
& poetry instead of budgets.
We row out across ragged waves
in my dory, coffee & beer
tucked under our seats, our poles
dangling treble hooks, those yellow-blooded
tube worms you hate
floating their unsuspecting red fronds
in our bait-can.

I let your Southern California eye
choose our bearings, the same place
where some great fish bent your pole
into the water, snapped the hook.
You lower the sledge-hammer anchor,
holding us to the thick bottom.
You whip a California cast, back
over your head, listen but do not watch.
Reach inside your jacket,
pull out a fat manila envelope.
From your father, you say, the latest Dodger
boxscores. First-class from Gardena
every week. Over my folded Sunday
sports page we talk about players retired
& traded from the Rams. Try to recall
who played right-field for the Cardinals
in '66; we get that specific.
Glance occasionally at our poles, the ferry,
the blue Olympics. You interrupt lines
from poems, Dodger batting averages,
with a bullhead, a flounder, ratfish
and a pollock—never the perch or rock cod
you want to cook for us, Chinese-style,
glazed and garnished with green onions
& parsley. You tell me about the Haku-kin girl
who came up after a reading and asked,
"Are you sure you aren't Chinese?"
Swearing at the memory, you act out
the joke, running out of room in the boat.

52

Outside the Dream Ritual

I wake up like a bird
under water. My left arm
is dead. I pick it up
at the elbow and straighten the bone.
Wanting to believe
in this reincarnation,
I squeeze back the slow blood,
hoping no clots are bumping their way
to my lungs. The wood
is thick under my skin.

I remember a radio program:
a 7-year-old boy watches a girl
his age, screaming
in the tumbling surf.
She somersaults away
from her name.
Forty years later he returns.
Waves are still memorizing
the shore. Kneeling
like a tribal woman
he looks inside the polished water,
sees the small bones
brushed white with age.

Lines for Fortune Cookies
—after Frank O'Hara

You have been smiling across the table at your date
with a sesame seed stuck in your teeth.
You will gain sophistication, write poems
and retire in Colfax, Washington.
Ever since you returned from the restroom
your zipper has revealed your Friday
nylon underwear.
You will never own a dog named Nose-mitten.
After your next wine hangover
a friend will take you out for breakfast
and order you a bulema with yogurt.
The next thermos bottle you see
will actually be a transistor radio
made in Japan.
You will become a prisoner in a sushi factory
and grow fat.
The person on your left
is stealing the last piece of barbecue pork.
In your next life you will be a teacher
and no one will ever call you by your real name.
The loud party at the next table
has just ordered stomach-lining fried in bean curd
without knowing better.
Someone at your table
secretly bites heads off gingerbread men.
All the people in this room
are glad that they are not you.

For the Ballerina in the Mojave Desert Who Has Painted Her Own Audience on a Canvas and Stretched It, Facing the Stage

There is no singing, no whispering or smoking.
Mozart spins off a record;
at the end of the music she spirals
into a statue. The canvas gallery,
the 16th Century Spanish court
she chose to perform for
silently applauds. Every seat
on the main floor & four balconies
is filled, faces with white smiles
shout, "Bravo . . . bravo!" Outside,
the one dusty street leads to San Francisco.
It leaves a general store with its gas pump,
weeds tumbling down the boardwalk,
only the ghosts of houses.

She bows, runs into the wings;
returns for an encore. Bows again
to the relentless applause of her art.

James Masao Mitsui is a Nisei (2nd generation Japanese-American) born 4 February 1940 in Skykomish, Washington. At the age of one he was moved with his family to the Tule Lake Relocation Camp in California. After 1½ years there his family moved to Lamona in eastern Washington where his father worked for the Great Northern Railway. In 1963 James Mitsui graduated from Eastern Washington State College where he played football and baseball. In 1975 he received an M.A. in English from the University of Washington. Currently he teaches at Lindbergh High School in Renton, Washington and lives on Bainbridge Island with his wife, Suzanne, and son, Tadao. His first book, JOURNAL OF THE SUN (Copper Canyon Press, 1974) received the Pacific Northwest Bookseller's Award.